WYDANIE NARODOWE
DZIEŁ FRYDERYKA CHOPINA

NATIONAL EDITION
OF THE WORKS OF FRYDERYK CHOPIN

# WALTZES
## Opp. 18, 34, 42, 64

NATIONAL EDITION
Edited by JAN EKIER

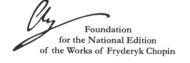

Foundation
for the National Edition
of the Works of Fryderyk Chopin

PWM
EDITION

SERIES A. WORKS PUBLISHED DURING CHOPIN'S LIFETIME. VOLUME XI

# FRYDERYK CHOPIN

## WALCE
### Op. 18, 34, 42, 64

WYDANIE NARODOWE
Redaktor naczelny: JAN EKIER

FUNDACJA WYDANIA NARODOWEGO
POLSKIE WYDAWNICTWO MUZYCZNE SA
WARSZAWA 2023

SERIA A. UTWORY WYDANE ZA ŻYCIA CHOPINA. TOM XI

Redakcja tomu: Jan Ekier, Paweł Kamiński

*Komentarz wykonawczy i Komentarz źródłowy (skrócony)* dołączone są do nut głównej
serii *Wydania Narodowego* oraz do strony internetowej www.chopin-nationaledition.com

Pełne *Komentarze źródłowe* do poszczególnych tomów wydawane są oddzielnie.

Wydany w oddzielnym tomie *Wstęp do Wydania Narodowego Dzieł Fryderyka Chopina
– 1. Zagadnienia edytorskie* obejmuje całokształt ogólnych problemów wydawniczych,
zaś *Wstęp... – 2. Zagadnienia wykonawcze* – całokształt ogólnych problemów interpretacyjnych.
Pierwsza część *Wstępu* jest także dostępna na stronie www.pwm.com.pl

*Walce* wydane pośmiertnie zawarte są w osobnym tomie (27 **B III**).

Editors of this Volume: Jan Ekier, Paweł Kamiński

A *Performance Commentary* and a *Source Commentary (abridged)* are included in the
music of the main series of the *National Edition* and available on www.chopin-nationaledition.com

Full *Source Commentaries* on each volume are published separately.

The *Introduction to the National Edition of the Works of Fryderyk Chopin*,
*1. Editorial Problems*, published as a separate volume, covers general matters concerning the publication.
The *Introduction... 2. Problems of Performance* covers all general questions of the interpretation.
First part of the *Introduction* is also available on the website www.pwm.com.pl

*Waltzes* published posthumously are contained in a separate volume (27 **B III**).

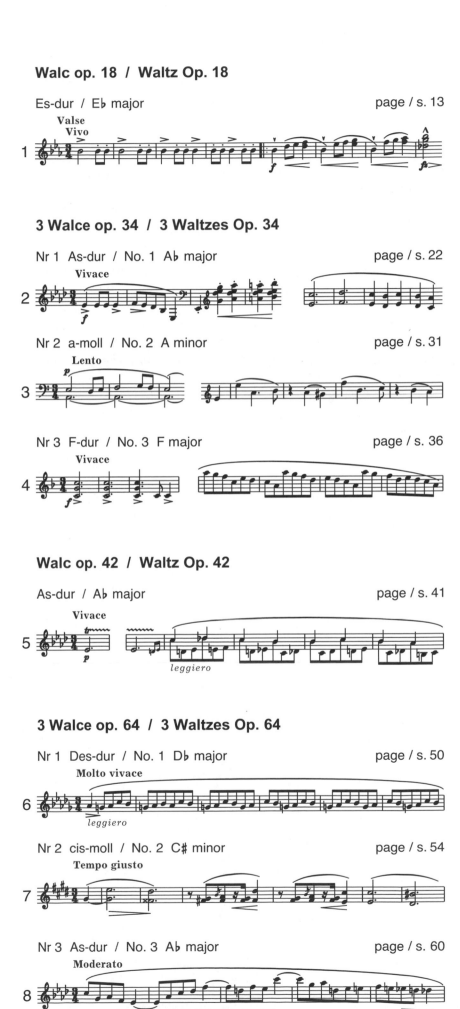

# o Walcach...

op. 18

„[Chopin] przepisuje Walca Es-dur z nową k o d ą, żeby go zanieść wydawcy i dostać p i e n i ą d z e
(bo mu ich brakuje) [...]"

Z listu Augusta Franchomme'a do Jules'a Forest, Paryż 11 maja 1834.

„Twoja siostra tyle była grzeczna, że mi swoją kompozycję przysłała. Ucieszyło mnie to niewymownie i zaraz
tego samego wieczora improwizowałem w jednym z tutejszych salonów na ładniuchny temat owej Maryni,
z którą się to w Pszennego domu za dawnych czasów po pokojach goniło... A dziś! Je prends la liberté
d'envoyer à mon estimable collègue Mlle Marie une petite valse que je viens de publier [Pozwalam sobie
przesłać mojej szanownej koleżance, pannie Marii, walczyka, który właśnie opublikowałem]. Oby setną cząstkę
przyjemności tej zrobił, jakiej ja doznałem odebrawszy wariacje."

Z listu F. Chopina do Feliksa Wodzińskiego w Genewie, Paryż 18 VII 1834.

op. 34

„Schlesinger jeszcze większy pies, żeby moje Walce w album kłaść! i Probstowi sprzedawać, kiedy ja
na jego żebranie dla Ojca mu do Berlina dałem."

Z listu F. Chopina do Juliana Fontany w Paryżu, Palma 28 XII 1838.

op. 34 nr 2

„Otóż i Valse mélancolique [– rzekł Chopin]. Widzi Pan, tego Walca nie zagra Pan nigdy w życiu, ale ponieważ
rozumie go Pan dobrze, chcę w nim Panu coś wpisać." [Następuje opis zamiany w t. 8 dwóch ćwierćnut
w prawej ręce, $d^1$ i $d^1$-$gis^1$ na $d^1$-$gis^1$-$c^2$ i $d^1$-$gis^1$-$h^1$, z zaznaczeniem, że zmiana ta brzmi pięknie również
przy powtórzeniach tego miejsca.]

Wilhelm von Lenz, *Die grossen Pianoforte-Virtuosen unserer Zeit*, Berlin 1872.

op. 42

„Ponieważ p. Pacini wydaje 30 bm. jeden z mych Walców w swoim zbiorze «Sto i jeden», czuję się w obowiązku przesłać Panom jedną odbitkę. Mam nadzieję, że wydanie nie napotka trudności [...]"

Z listu F. Chopina do firmy Breitkopf i Härtel w Lipsku, Paryż 18 VI 1840.

„Ten Walc, wykluwający się z ośmiotaktowego trylu, należy oddać – jak mawiał Chopin – na modłę zegarowego kuranta. Wykonywany przez niego, uosabiał w bezustannym stretta-prestissimo, z zachowaniem taktu w basie, szczyt Chopinowskiego stylu rubato. Girlanda kwiatów, tancerek i tancerzy!"

Wilhelm von Lenz, *Uebersichtliche Beurtheilung der Pianoforte-Kompositionen von Chopin [...]*, „Neue Berliner Musikzeitung" 18 IX 1872.

op. 64 nr 1

„W pierwszym Walcu [...] z początkowych czterech taktów robił Chopin w przybliżeniu dwa; «to winno rozwijać się jak [nić] z kłębka» mawiał. Takt [Walca] wchodził wraz z basem w piątym takcie."

Wilhelm von Lenz, *Uebersichtliche [...]*

„Pewna wytworna dama, obecna na ostatnim koncercie Chopina w Paryżu (1848), na którym grał między innymi swojego Walca Des-dur, chciała poznać sekret, dzięki któremu wykonywane przez niego na fortepianie gamy były tak potoczyste [le secret de Chopin pour que les gammes fussent si coulées sur le piano]. Relacjonująca mi to pani Dubois dodała, że to wyrażenie szczęśliwie oddawało ową nieporównanie delikatną przejrzystość [jego gry]."

Fryderyk Niecks, *Frederick Chopin as a Man and Musician*, Londyn 1888.

op. 64 nr 2

„Trudno było zadowolić Chopina w tym Walcu. Tylko on umiał [właściwie] połączyć jedyną (!) szesnastkę w trzecim takcie z następującą po niej ćwierćnutą."

Wilhelm von Lenz, *Uebersichtliche [...]*

# about the Waltzes...

Op. 18

"[Chopin] rewrites his Waltz in E♭ with a new coda, to bring it to the publisher and receive the money (because he lacks it) [...]"

From a letter by Auguste Franchomme to Jules Forest, Paris 11 May 1834.

"Your sister was so kind as to send me her composition, causing me great joy. Immediately the same evening I improvised in one of the local salons on a pretty theme by the same Marynia, with whom I used to play chase in the house of Pszenny in olden days... And today! Je prends la liberté d'envoyer à mon estimable collègue Mlle Marie une petite valse que je viens de publier [I take the liberty of sending my honourable colleague, Miss Maria, a little waltz which I had just published]. May it bring her but one hundredth of the pleasure which I experienced upon receiving the variations."

From a letter by F. Chopin to Feliks Wodziński in Geneva, Paris 18 July 1834.

Op. 34

"Schlesinger is even more of a dog to include my Waltzes into an album! and to sell them to Probst, when I, at his entreatment, sent them to his Father in Berlin."

From a letter by F. Chopin to Julian Fontana in Paris, Palma 28 December 1838.

Op. 34, no. 2

"Here is the Valse mélancolique [—said Chopin]. You see that You shall never play it as long as you live, but since You understand it well I wish to add something into it." [The succeeding description concerns the change in bar 8 of two crotchets in the right hand, $d^1$ and $d^1$-$g\#^1$ into $d^1$-$g\#^1$-$c^2$ and $d^1$-$g\#^1$-$b^1$, stressing the fact that this change sounds equally beautiful in repetitions of the passage.]

Wilhelm von Lenz, *Die grossen Pianoforte-Virtuosen unserer Zeit*, Berlin 1872.

Op. 42

*"Since on the 30th of this month Mr. Pacini publishes one of my Waltzes in his collection 'Hundred and One' I am obliged to send You a copy. I hope that the edition will not encounter obstacles [...]"*

From a letter by F. Chopin to the firm Breitkopf & Härtel in Leipzig, Paris 18 June 1840.

*"Chopin used to say that this Waltz, stemming from an eight-bar trill, should be rendered in the fashion of a chiming clock. Played by him, its incessant Stretta-Prestissimo, with a retention of the time in the bass, personified the peak of the Chopinesque rubato style. A floral garland of dancers!"*

Wilhelm von Lenz, *Uebersichtliche Beurtheilung der Pianoforte-Kompositionen von Chopin [...]*, "Neue Berliner Musikzeitung" 18 September 1872.

Op. 64, no. 1

*"In the first Waltz [...] Chopin turned the four beginning bars into approximately two; 'it should unravel like [thread] from a ball' he used to say. The time [of the Waltz] was introduced together with the bass in the fifth bar."*

Wilhelm von Lenz, *Uebersichtliche [...]*

*"A great lady who was present at Chopin's last concert in Paris (1848), when he played among other works his Valse in D flat, wished to know 'le secret de Chopin pour que les gammes fussent si coulées sur le piano' [Chopin's secret for the scales were so flowing on the piano]. Madame Dubois who related this incident to me, added that the expression was felicitous, for this 'limpidité délicate' had never been equalled."*

Frederick Niecks, *Frederick Chopin as a Man and Musician*, London 1888.

Op. 64, no. 2

*"It was difficult to satisfy Chopin in this Waltz. Only he was capable of linking [properly] the only (!) semiquaver in the third bar with the succeeding crotchet."*

Wilhelm von Lenz, *Uebersichtliche [...]*

# Valse brillante

*A Mademoiselle Laura Horsford*

op. 18

** Palcowanie Chopinowskie w tym *Walcu* pochodzi w całości z egzemplarzy lekcyjnych.
Chopin's fingering in this *Waltz* comes entirely from pupils' copies.

16

* W źródłach prawdopodobnie błędnie dwa razy *f¹* zamiast *d¹* w akordach. Patrz *Komentarz źródłowy.*
  The sources have, probably mistakenly, *f¹* twice instead of *d¹* in the chords. *Vide Source Commentary.*

19

# Trois valses

## Nº 1

*A Mademoiselle J. de Thun Hohenstein*

op. 34 nr 1

* Inny podział pomiędzy ręce - patrz *Komentarz wykonawczy*.
For a different division between hands - *vide Performance Commentary*.

FWN 11 **A XI**

* Dźwięk *as²* należy powtórzyć.
  The note *ab²* should be repeated.

* Dźwięk *as²* należy powtórzyć.
  The note *ab²* should be repeated.

26

FWN 11 **A XI**

28

* W źródłach ostatnią ósemką jest prawdopodobnie błędnie *f²*. Patrz *Komentarz źródłowy*.
The sources have, probably mistakenly, *f²* as the last quaver. *Vide Source Commentary*.

29

30

# № 2

*A Madame la Baronne C. d'Ivry*

# № 3

*A Mademoiselle A. d'Eichthal*

**Vivace**

op. 34 nr 3

38

* W źródłach ostatnią ćwierćnutą jest prawdopodobnie błędnie 𝄢 . Patrz *Komentarz źródłowy.*
  In the sources the last crotchet is, probably mistakenly, . Vide *Source Commentary.*

# Valse

op. 42

* Patrz *Komentarz źródłowy.*
 *Vide Source Commentary.*

** Dopuszczalny wariant jak w t. 44, 52, 76, 84.
 Permissible variant as in bars 44, 52, 76, 84.

FWN 11 **A XI**

* Nieco inna, skromniejsza brzmieniowo i dynamicznie, autentyczna wersja zakończenia *Walca*:
  A slightly different, authentic version of the end of the *Waltz*, more modest in sonority and dynamics:

** Autentyczny wariant:
   Authentic variant:

49

# Trois valses

## № 1

*A Madame la Comtesse Delphine Potocka*

op. 64 nr 1

# FRYDERYK CHOPIN
# WALTZES

Performance Commentary
Source Commentary (abridged)

# PERFORMANCE COMMENTARY

## Notes on the musical text

The v a r i a n t s marked as *ossia* were given this label by Chopin or
were added in his hand to pupils' copies; variants without this designation are the result of discrepancies in the texts of authentic versions or
an inability to establish an unambiguous reading of the text.
Minor authentic alternatives (single notes, ornaments, slurs, accents,
pedal indications, etc.) that can be regarded as variants are enclosed in
round brackets (), whilst editorial additions are written in square brackets [].
Pianists who are not interested in editorial questions, and want to base
their performance on a single text, unhampered by variants, are rec-
ommended to use the music printed in the principal staves, including all
the markings in brackets.
Chopin's original fingering is indicated in large bold-type numerals,
**1 2 3 4 5,** in contrast to the editors' fingering which is written in small
italic numerals *1 2 3 4 5*. Wherever authentic fingering is enclosed in
parentheses this means that it was not present in the primary sources,
but added by Chopin to his pupils' copies. The dashed signs indicating
the distribution of parts between the hands come from the editors.
A general discussion on the interpretation of Chopin's works is to be
contained in a separate volume: *The Introduction to the National Edition*, in the section entitled *Problems of Performance*.

Abbreviations: R.H. — right hand, L.H. — left hand.

## 1. Waltz in E flat major, Op. 18

p. 13

*Bars 12, 36, 44, 165, 167 and 169* L.H. Slurs in parentheses
(cf. *Source Commentary*) stress the necessity of sustaining the
fundamental bass note. Obviously, it is necessary to do the same
wherever indicated by the rhythmic value of the bass note.

p. 16

*Bar 118 and analog.* R.H. The grace-notes can be executed both
in an anticipatory manner or on the downbeat (the first one simultaneously with *Db* in the L.H. and *f¹* in the R.H.).

p. 17

*Bars 133–148 and 245–258* R.H. It is not essential whether the
grace-notes are sounded simultaneously with the crotchets in the
L.H. or slightly earlier. Greater importance is attached to their
sound merit — they should be lighter than the crotchets creating
the melodic line.

p. 18

*Bars 165–180* The markings *p* borrowed from the pupils' copies
in bars 167 and 171 and *una corda* in bars 179–180 suggest
a performance conception consisting in a dialogue between pairs
of bars imbued with different expression: more vivid in bars 165–
166 and 169–170 and gentler in bars 167–168 and 171–172.
A similar dialogue is found in *Mazurka in C minor*, Op. 30, no. 1,
bars 1–16, *Mazurka in B minor*, Op. 30, no. 2, bars 1–16 and
*Nocturne in B*, Op. 32, no.1, bars 27–30.

p. 21

*Bar 287* The sign 🎵, introduced by Chopin into the pupils' copy,
probably denotes sustaining the pedal until the end of the *Waltz*.

## 2. Waltz in A flat major, Op. 34, no. 1

The autograph of the original edition of the *Waltz* contains more performance markings than the final version. Some of them contradict
later indications, others refer to fragments substantially changed by
Chopin afterwards. The markings listed below can be regarded as an
expressive supplement to the final version:

| | |
|---|---|
| bars 13–16 | *veloce e con forza* |
| bar 17 | *con anima* |
| bars 33 and 193 | *leggiero* |
| bars 49 and 209 | *f, risoluto* |

| | |
|---|---|
| bars 50, 54, 210 and 214 | *cresc.* |
| bars 57 and 217 | *ff* |
| bars 58–60 and 218–220 | *appassionato* |
| bar 81 and analog. | *dolce* |
| bar 95 and analog. | *dim.* ⟞ |
| bar 113 | *dolente* |
| bar 121 | *ff, appassionato* |
| bars 127–128 | *smorzando e rall.* |
| bar 145 | *risoluto* |
| bars 146–152 | *sempre più forte ed animato* |
| bar 177 | *dolce e tranquillo.* |

p. 22

*Bars 11 and 12* A different division between hands:

*Bar 16* The last four quavers can be executed with the L.H.,
which makes possible a convenient preparation of the right hand
for the entry of the theme in the next bar.

*Bars 26 and 186* R.H. The slur next to the grace-note can be

understood either as a conventional sign or as an arpeggio: 𝄽
The editors recommend to perform the ornament in an anticipatory
manner, similarly to the mode suggested by Chopin for the grace-
note in bars 28–29.

p. 24

*Bars 67–68 and analog.* R.H. The notation of the runs in the
sources does not indicate distinctly the moment of their beginning. The following performance appears to be the easiest:

With suitably dexterous fingers it is possible to begin the figuration slightly later, e.g.:

Analogously in remaining places.
The *ossia* variants in bars 163–164 and 167–168 are best executed in the following manner:

Regardless of the selected rhythmic solution it is necessary to
avoid accentuating the notes of passages corresponding to particular crotchets of the accompaniment.

p. 30

*Bar 300* The intention of the execution of bars 300–305 on
a single pedal, foreseen by Chopin, is to retain the sonority of the
Ab-major chord from bar 300 also in following bars. The change
of the pedal on the last crotchet, proposed by the editors, makes
it possible to attain this goal without mingling the retained harmony with the dissonant notes *d¹* and *f¹*.

### 3. Waltz in A minor, Op. 34, no. 2

p. 31    *Bars 1–16 and analog.* L.H. The fingering in brackets proposed by Chopin is a particular example of the "expressive fingering" in which Chopin entrusted the long melodic notes (minims), which simultaneously comprise expressively important harmonic notes, to the first finger.

p. 32    *Bars 55, 59, 63 and analog.* R.H. Double grace-notes should be executed similarly to mordents (cf. *Source Commentary*), sounding the first simultaneously with the bass note. In the opinion of the editors the difference in the notation (♫ and ♫) does not denote a distinction of the performance.

### 4. Waltz in F major, Op. 34, no. 3

p. 36    *Bars 1–9* The division of chords between hands, as noted by Chopin, suggests arpeggiating them in the L.H.; the arpeggios should be anticipated ($e^1$ sounded together with the R.H.).

p. 38    *Bars 83–84, 87–88 and analog.* R.H. See commentary to *Waltz in E♭*, Op. 18, bars 133–148 and 245–258.

   *Bars 93 and 109* R.H. Beginning of the trill:  $d^2$ simultaneously with *c* in the L.H.

### 5. Waltz in A flat major, Op. 42

p. 41    *Bars 9–40 and analog.* R.H. The slur over those bars suggests a *legato possibile* execution of the theme melody written in crotchets. The marking *leggiero* refers probably to the quaver figuration. See *Source Commentary*.

p. 45    *Bar 158* R.H. The arpeggio with the grace-note should be executed analogously as in bar 160 (see below).

   *Bar 160* R.H. The first grace-note ($f^1$) should be struck simultaneously with E♭ in the L.H.

p. 47    *Bar 216* L.H. In this bar, owing to different harmonic succession, the use of the variant version of the accompaniment (as in bar 44, 52 and analog.) is inadmissible.

p. 49    *Bars 281-282* R.H. In the editors' opinion it is better, for practical reasons, to choose one of the two versions in which bar 282 is an exact transposition of bar 281 (fourth quavers of both bars have either thirds or single notes).

### 6. Waltz in D flat major, Op. 64, no. 1

p. 50    *Bars 1–4* The description by Chopin's pupil W. von Lenz (see quotations *about the Waltzes...*, prior to the musical text) seems to suggest that Chopin himself performed this introduction freely, beginning with a tempo quicker than the actual tempo of the *Waltz*. This account could depict one of the ways in which Chopin played the *Waltz*, which today it would be difficult to emulate upon the basis of such a general description. The fact that all the sources have verbal markings in bar 1, without any changes in bar 5, as well as the presence of the annotation "4 mesures" in the pupils' copy indicate rather a performance conception of the beginning of the *Waltz*, concurrent with the metre.

p. 52    *Bars 69–72* R.H. The sign ***tr***, repeated four times, probably denotes a continuos four bar-long trill (see *Source Commentary* to those bars and the variant beginning of the *Waltz*).

p. 53    *Bars 121–123* R.H. The sign which in bar 123 recommends to sound $a^1$ together with A♭ in the L.H., added to a pupil's copy, suggests the following rhythmic grouping of the passage:

### 7. Waltz in C sharp minor, Op. 64, no. 2

The relation of the t e m p i of the initial section of the *Waltz* (bars 1–32 and analog.) and the successive figurative section (bars 33–64 and analog.) gives rise to doubts (see *Source Commentary* to bars 33 and 161). In the editors' opinion an analysis of the agogic markings leads to the following practical conclusions:
— **Tempo giusto** at the beginning of the Waltz denotes a certain sphere of a tempo proper for this dance, encompassing both the moderate cantilene tempo of the opening section and the slightly quicker tempo of the figurative section,
— all agogic markings should be understood flexibly, without a distinct contrasting of the tempi,
— in bars 49–64 and analog., the marking ***pp***, the absence of recurrent signs ═══ and long slurs suggest a dance-like light and very regular performance.
Obviously, the proportions of the tempi and other interpretation elements depend on the discretion of the performer; this Waltz, containing a gamut of expressive hues, offers great opportunities for the invention of the pianist.

p. 54    *Bars 3–4 and analog.* R.H. According to Chopin (see quotations *about the Waltzes...* prior to the musical text) it is necessary to differentiate clearly the value of the quaver, which begins the motif, from the subsequent value of the semiquaver. Cf. similar rhythmic figures in *Waltz in A♭*, Op. 34, no. 1, bars 60–63 and analog.

   *Bars 27–28, 29–30 and analog.* R.H. The sources contain the following three combinations of a repetition and retention of notes in those bars:

On the other hand, the sources lack a version with a repetition of $c\#^2$ in bar 28 and the retention of $b^1$ in bars 29–30. In bars 155–158 it is possible to repeat the version chosen for bars 27–30 or to apply another of the above versions.

p. 56    *Bars 65–96* R.H. Chopin noted down two rhythmic-expressive conceptions of this section: one (main text), which repeats notes at the beginning of bars 67, 71, 77 and 93, and the other (variants), which sustains appropriate notes (cf. *Source Commentary* to bars 66-67, 70-71, 76-77 and 92-93). In the opinion of the editors, the performer might select variants, e.g. a repetition of $eb^2$ in bar 67 and $f^2$ in bar 71, and the sustaining of $db^3$ in bars 76-77 and 92-93.

   *Bar 88* R.H. The first grace-note, $c^2$, should be sounded simultaneously with the fifth $c^1$–$gb^1$ in the L.H.

### 8. Waltz in A flat major, Op. 64, no. 3

p. 63    *Bar 109* R.H. The grace-note should be sounded simultaneously with A♭ in the L.H.

*Jan Ekier, Paweł Kamiński*

# SOURCE COMMENTARY /ABRIDGED/

## Introductory comments

The following commentary sets out in an abridged form the principles of editing the musical text of particular works and discusses the most important discrepancies between the authentic sources; furthermore, it draws attention to unauthentic versions which are most frequently encountered in the collected editions of Chopin's music compiled after his death. A separately published *Source Commentary* contains a detailed description of the sources, their filiation, justification of the choice of primary sources, a thorough presentation of the differences between them and a reproduction of characteristic fragments.

Abbreviations: R.H. – right hand, L.H. – left hand. The sign → symbolises a connection between sources; it should be read "and ... based on it".

## Remark to the second edition

In the course of preparing this edition of *Waltzes* attention was paid to an important, heretofore unknown source to *Waltz in A♭*, Op. 42 – a proof copy of the first French edition with corrections and supplements in Chopin's hand*. Furthermore, several variants have been added to the musical text thanks to editorial clarifications suggested by Dr. Krzysztof Grabowski of Paris.

## Titles of Waltzes

The original titles of the *Waltzes*, preceding the musical text, are cited according to the autographs. The designations 'grande' (Opp. 18, 34, 42), 'brillante' (Op. 34) and 'nouvelle' (Op. 42), occurring in the original editions, are probably an arbitrary addition made by the publishers.

## 1. Waltz in E flat major, Op. 18

Sources
**AI**  Autograph/fair-copy of the original version, dedicated to Miss Horsford in Paris, 10 July 1833 (Yale University, New Haven). It differs from the ultimate version as regards many details, particular sections (which in the final version correspond to bars 5–68, 69–116, 117–164) are numbered as consecutive waltzes, without coda.
**AII**  Autograph/fair-copy, details close to the final version; without coda (Fryderyk Chopin Museum, Warsaw).
**A**  Autograph/fair-copy of the final version, serving as the basis for the first French edition (Musée de Mariemont).
**FE1**  First French edition, M. Schlesinger (M.S. 1599), Paris June 1834, based on **A** and twice corrected by Chopin.
**FE2**  Second impression of **FE1** (same firm and number), in which Chopin corrected, i.a. details of pedalling and articulation.
**FE3**  Third impression of **FE1**, H. Lemoine (2777.HL), Paris December 1842. The **FE3** musical text does not differ from **FE2**.
**FE**  = **FE1**, **FE2** and **FE3**.
**FE4**  Second French edition, H. Lemoine (3611.HL), about 1850, introducing, i.a. a number of arbitrary changes of performance markings, accepted by some of the later collected editions.
**FE5**  Reprint of **FE4**, H. Lemoine (5344.HL), about 1859.
**FED, FED', FES, FEJ, FEX** — pupils' copies of **FE** with annotations by Chopin, containing fingering, performance directives, variants, corrections of printing errors:

---

* The editors of the National Edition wish to express their gratitude to Prof. **Paul Badura-Skoda** of Vienna for rendering available a photocopy of this recently discovered source.

**FED, FED'** — two copies (**FE3, FE2**) from a collection belonging to Chopin's pupil Camille Dubois (Bibliothèque Nationale, Paris),
**FES** — copy of **FE2** from a collection belonging to Chopin's pupil Jane Stirling (Bibliothèque Nationale, Paris),
**FEJ** — copy of **FE3** from a collection belonging to Chopin's sister Ludwika Jędrzejewicz (Fryderyk Chopin Museum, Warsaw),
**FEX** — copy of **FE1** of unknown provenance (Ewa & Jeremiusz Glensk collection, Poznań). The pencil annotations it contains display characteristic features of Chopin's teaching notes.
**GE1**  First German edition, Breitkopf & Härtel (5545), Leipzig July 1834, based on the proofs of **FE1** without Chopin's final corrections. **GE1** contains traces of publisher's adjustments and was not corrected by Chopin.
**GE2**  Second German edition (same firm and number), after 1840, basically re-creating the text of **GE1**, with several distinct errors, and supplementing chromatic signs.
**GE3**  Third German edition (same firm and number), introducing a number of arbitrary changes.
**GE4, GE5** — fourth German edition, Breitkopf & Härtel (9618), about 1858, re-creating the slightly changed text of **GE3**, and its later (after 1872) revised impression.
**GE**  = **GE1, GE2, GE3, GE4** and **GE5**.
**EE1**  First English edition, Wessel & C° (W & C° 1157), London August 1834, based on the proofs of **FE1**, without Chopin's final corrections. **EE1** contains traces of publisher's revision and was not corrected by Chopin.
**EE2**  Second impression of **EE1** (same firm and number), introducing further unauthentic changes and supplementation.
**EE**  = **EE1** and **EE2**.

Editorial Principles
We accept as our basis **FE2** as the latest authentic source, compared with **A** and **AII**. We take into consideration Chopin's annotations in five pupils' copies. Isolated, obvious oversights of performance markings (slurs, accents, staccato dots) are supplemented according to **AII** and analogous passages in the final version (**A** and **FE**).

The Chopin fingering comes from all five pupils' copies (predominantly from **FED'**). In recurring fragments the fingering is frequently repeated partly or as a whole, testifying to the importance attached to it by Chopin. Nonetheless, the composer prepared the *Waltz* for print without the fingering; thus, in order not to overburden the text, we give all the numerals referring to the given place already upon the first occasion, without repeating them later.

p. 13
*Bars 1–4* R.H. The octave doubling of the introduction given in the footnote was marked by Chopin in **FED'**. The introduction is noted in octaves also in **AI**, which additionally contains the marking *f*.

*Bar 5* In **FE** (→**GE,EE**) there is no *f* marking, probably due to an oversight by the engraver.

*Bars 5–7, 10–12 & analog.* **FE4** arbitrarily replaced authentic signs ⏜ in bars 5–7 & analog. by a single sign spanning 3 bars. Similarly, in bars 10–12 & analog. it introduced a 3-bar sign ⏝.

*Bars 12, 36, 44, 165, 167 & 169* L.H. Slurs next to the bass notes come from **FED'** (all) and **FEX** (in bars 165-169). In **FED'** such a slur is found also in bar 66 but we do not give it due to its possible misreading as a tie sustaining *e♭*.

*Bar 28* L.H. At the beginning of the bar, **A** (→**FE**→**GE,EE**) has *a♭* as a crotchet. We accept the notation of the accompaniment in analogous bars, where Chopin lengthened the rhythmic value of this note: in bar 60 in **A** and in bar 212 in the proofs of **FE2**.

p. 15
*Bar 69* The designation *dolce* is found in autographs but not in the original editions.

4

<sup>p. 17</sup> *Bars 142-144* R.H. The *ossia* variant given in the footnote was added by Chopin into **FE**X.

*Bars 145–146* R.H. The fingering inscribed into **FE**X present difficulties in interpretation:  . It is unclear how to supplement it, and moreover, both figures could possibly refer to the neighbouring grace-notes. For this reason we give only the fingering of **FE**D' which raises no doubt.

*Bar 156* R.H. In **A**, **GE** and **EE** the quaver is the sixth *f¹–db².* In **A**, similar figures in bars 121–124 show the deletion of the lower note of the sixth; the retention of *f¹* is an oversight by Chopin, corrected in the second proof-reading of **FE**1.

<sup>p. 18</sup> *Bars 167, 171 and 179–180* The sign *p* in bars 167 and 171 comes from **FE**D'. In bars 179–180 it contains the sign with which Chopin marked the use of the left pedal in **FE**S of *Nocturne in F#,* Op. 15 no. 2. See *Performance Commentary* to bars 165–180.

*Bars 173* R.H. The *tenuto* signs come from **FE**X.

*Bars 177–180* R.H. The *ossia* variant given in the footnote was added by Chopin into **FE**X.

*Bar 178* L.H. **A** (→**FE**1→**EE**,**GE**1→**GE**2) has no ♮ before the lower note of the second crotchet. This error was corrected by Chopin in the proofs of **FE**2. **GE**3 (→**GE**4→**GE**5) arbitrarily introduced the version of bars 166, 170 and 174 into this bar. **GE**5 erroneously introduced the correct version of bar 178 into bar 174.

*Bars 183–185* R.H. The *ossia* variant given in the footnote was added by Chopin into **FE**J; the same version is given in **A**II.

<sup>p. 19</sup> *Bar 224* L.H. On the second crotchet **A** (→**FE**1→**GE**,**EE**) has *eb¹* in the chord. During the proof-reading of **FE**2 Chopin changed it to *db¹* (as in analogous bars).

*Bar 231* L.H. In analogous bars 191 and 199 in **A**, Chopin changed *f¹* to *d¹* in the chords. The retention of *f¹* was almost certainly unintentional (when correcting Chopin often missed one of several similar passages).

<sup>p. 21</sup> *Bar 274* L.H. On the second and third crotchet **A** originally had a three-note chord *Bb–eb–g.* Subsequently, Chopin deleted and replaced it with a *Bb–g* sixth. Ultimately, he added *eb,* but only on the second crotchet of the bar; this version was published in **FE**1 (→**GE**,**EE**). In the proofs of **FE**2 Chopin added *eb* also on the last crotchet, thus returning to the original conception.

*Bars 277–278* R.H. **GE** and **EE** erroneously have ♭ before the first *c²* in bar 277. Distinct naturals in **A** and **FE** leave no doubt as to Chopin's intention. **GE**2 and subsequent German editions arbitrarily added ♭ also prior to *c²* in bar 278.

*Bar 278* L.H. **FE**4 and the majority of later collected editions arbitrarily added *eb* to the sixth on the second and third crotchet.

*Bar 279* R.H. Prior to *d¹* at the beginning of the bar **A** has a superfluous ♮, which the engraver of **FE** misread as ♭. This error was transferred from the proofs of **FE** to **EE** and **GE** (not corrected until **GE**5). The erroneous and unnecessary sign was removed in the final proof-reading of **FE**1.

*Bar 287* In **FE**D Chopin added the sign of depressing the pedal.

*Bar 304* This bar, added by Chopin in **A**, but initially overlooked by the engraver of **FE**, does not occur in **GE** or **EE**. Chopin supplemented this gap in the final proof-reading of **FE**1.

*Bar 307* L.H. **GE** does not have the lower *Eb₁.*

## 2. Waltz in A flat major, Op. 34, no. 1

S o u r c e s
**AI**   Autograph/fair-copy of an earlier version of the *Waltz,* written on 15 September 1835 in Děčin (Tetschen) in an album of the Countesses von Thun-Hohenstein (lost, photocopy in the Fryderyk Chopin Museum, Warsaw). In comparison with the final version, its characteristic feature is a larger number of performance markings, written probably with an amateur pianist in mind.
**A**   Autograph of the final version, serving as the basis for the first French edition (Warsaw Music Society). In comparison to the earlier **AI** edition, in **A** Chopin added a coda and changed many melodic-rhythmic and harmonic details.
**FE**   First French edition, M. Schlesinger (M.S. 2715), Paris December 1838, based on **A** and twice corrected, presumably by Julian Fontana. It is highly probable that Chopin took part in the proof-reading.
**FE**D, **FE**S — as in *Waltz in Eb,* Op. 18.
**GE**1   First German edition, Breitkopf & Härtel (6032), Leipzig December 1838, based on the proofs of **FE** which did not contain the final corrections made by Chopin. **GE**1 includes a number of obvious errors and contains traces of publisher's adjustments; it was not corrected by Chopin. There are copies of **GE**1 with different covers.
**GE**2   Second German edition, Breitkopf & Härtel (9620), about 1858, with a detailed revision of the text of **GE**1 (correction of errors and numerous changes intent on a uniformisation of analogous passages).
**GE**3   Later (after 1872) impression of **GE**2, with further slight changes.
**GE**   = **GE**1, **GE**2 and **GE**3.
**EE**1   First English edition, Wessel & C° (W & C° 2280), London December 1838, based on **FE** and including a number of adjustments; it was not corrected by Chopin.
**EE**2   Second impression of **EE**1, with slight supplements.
**EE**   = **EE**1 and **EE**2.

E d i t o r i a l   P r i n c i p l e s
We accept as our basis **A**. The supplements and changes in **FE**, which could have been introduced by Chopin and were accepted by him during lessons, are given in the main text, with the **A** version added in the variants. We take into consideration also Chopin's annotations in pupils' copies. Pedal markings come from **A**, **AI** and **FE**; we give in parentheses signs occurring only in **FE** and those among the signs contained in **AI**, whose transference to the final version could give rise to objections owing to textural or harmonic differences between the two versions. Other performance markings in **AI**, which can be regarded as proposals supplementing the final version, are given in the *Performance Commentary.*

<sup>p. 22</sup> *Bar 26 and analog.* R.H. In bar 26 the flat lowering *g¹* to *gb¹* was added in the proofs of **FE** (→**GE**,**EE**). This change should certainly occur also in bar 186, and thus we give this version in both passages. The variant comes from **A** and **AI**. Stylistically, both versions are possible: similar harmonic turns are encountered in, e.g. *Waltz in Gb,* WN 42, bar 28 (a version from the Yale autograph) and *in Eb,* Op. 18, bar 178. The slur over the grace-note (conventional or denoting an arpeggio) is given according to **A**. In **FE** (→**GE**,**EE**) it is placed below the heads of notes, mistakenly tying *gb¹.*

*Bar 29 and analog.* R.H. In **A** the grace-note is written before the bar line. In **FE** (→**GE**1,**EE**) this notation is repeated only in bar 29; in bar 189 the grace-note is placed mistakenly behind the bar line. In **GE**2 this erroneous version was employed in both bars.

<sup>p. 23</sup> *Bar 40 and analog.* R.H. We give the sign *tr* according to **A**. In **FE** (→**GE**,**EE**) it was deciphered as ∿. **AI** has *tr* both here and in bar 32.

*Bar 48 (prima volta) and 176–177* R.H. Some of the later collected editions arbitrarily added a tie sustaining note *eb¹.*

*Bar 62 and analog.* L.H. On the second crotchet **GE**1 (→**GE**2) mistakenly repeats the first chord of the bar.

<sup>p. 24</sup> *Bars 67, 71 and analog.* R.H. Some of the later collected editions have trills instead of mordents. Their presence has a counterpart in **AI**, although in that particular autograph corresponding motifs

have a different, more richly ornamented form, both in bars 50–51 and here. The final version of A (→FE→GE,EE) has distinct mordents, and bars 163 and 167 even show deletions of the *tr* signs.

*Bar 69* L.H. In the chord on the second crotchet FE (→GE1, EE) mistakenly has *ab* instead of *bb*.

*Bar 83 and analog.* L.H. In A Chopin changed the number and rhythm of strokes in the top voice. In FE (→GE,EE) one of the ensuing deletions was misread as a tie joining both *ab*.

p. 26 *Bars 163–164 and 167–168* R.H. The pencilled signs added in FED over the ends of the passages presumably denote the possibility of extending them by an octave, which we have taken into consideration as *ossia*. Such an interpretation can be supported by AI, in which the second passage is written up to $c^4$.

p. 27 *Bar 171* L.H. On the second crotchet A (→FE→GE,EE1) has $ab^1$ instead of $gb^1$ in the chord. The error made by Chopin is testified by ♭ on the level of $gb^1$, which is unjustified next to $ab^1$.

*Bar 175* R.H. FE (→GE,EE) overlooked $c^1$ in the last chord.

*Bar 189* L.H. FE (→GE1,EE) overlooked $eb^1$ in the chords.

p. 29 *Bars 239–240 and 243–244* R.H. FE (→GE,EE) overlooked ties sustaining $f^2$.

*Bar 243* L.H. In GE the lowest note in the chord on the second crotchet is mistakenly *f*.

*Bar 244* R.H. In A the top note in the first chord is mistakenly $db^3$. R.H. FE (→GE,EE) overlooked the point lengthening $ab^2$.

*Bar 247* R.H. The last quaver in A (→FE→GE1,EE) is $f^2$. The mistake, probably made by Chopin, is indicated by:
— $eb^3$ in bar 255; this type of variegation of virtuoso figuration, difficult to capture sonorically, is rather unlikely,
— a possible mechanical error in writing similar bars 245–247,
— the smoother sound of $eb^2$, especially together with the line of accented top notes in the L.H.

*Bar 262 and 264* R.H. The main text comes from FE (→GE,EE), and the variants – from A. The absence of naturals in A cannot be regarded as an obvious oversight on the part of Chopin; in a similar context Chopin treated the melodic voice regardless of the harmony – it can contain both the chord sound (raised) or its not raised counterpart. *Cf.* e. g. *Etude in C minor*, Op. 10 no. 12, bars 33-35 & 76, and *in F minor*, Dbop. 36 no. 1, bars 40, 42, 46.

p. 30 *Bars 272–273* L.H. FE (→GE,EE) overlooked a tie sustaining *f*.

*Bar 286* L.H. At the beginning of the bar FE (→GE,EE) has *Eb*. This is probably a mistake committed by the engraver, as testified by a comparison of the bass line and the entire harmonic context in bars 277–284 and 285–292.

*Bars 303–304* Between those bars A contained two other bars, which Chopin ultimately deleted. However, he left, probably due to carelessness, a 🎵 sign referring to one of the deleted bars. In FE (→GE,EE) this sign was unnecessarily placed in bar 304 with the additional sign ❄ in bar 303. In FES Chopin crossed out both signs.

## 3. Waltz in A minor, Op. 34, no. 2

### Sources

A  Autograph serving as the basis for the first French edition (inaccessible, photocopy in the Fryderyk Chopin Museum, Warsaw).

FE1  First French edition, M. Schlesinger (M.S. 2716), Paris December 1838, based on A and twice corrected, presumably by Julian Fontana. It is highly probable that Chopin took part in the proof-reading.

FE2  Second French edition, Brandus et Cⁱᵉ (B. et Cⁱᵉ 2716), Paris 1854–1858, re-creating, with some errors, the text of FE1.

FE  = FE1 and FE2.

FED, FES, FEJ — as in *Waltz in Eb*, Op. 18.

GE1  First German edition, Breitkopf & Härtel (6033), Leipzig December 1838, based most probably on the proofs of FE1. GE1 includes a number of obvious errors and contains traces of publisher's adjustment; it was not corrected by Chopin. There are copies of GE1 with different covers (three versions).

GE2  Second German edition (same firm and number), after 1852, with numerous modifications in relation to GE1 (corrected errors, changed slurs and other arbitrary changes).

GE3  Third German edition (same firm and number), after 1858, with further arbitrary changes.

GE  = GE1, GE2 and GE3.

EE  First English edition, Wessel & C° (W & C° 2281), London December 1838, based on FE and including a number of adjustments; it was not corrected by Chopin. There are copies with different covers and title pages.

The copy written by George Sand (photocopy in the Fryderyk Chopin Museum, Warsaw) and a fragment of a copy by an unknown copyist (Österreichische Nationalbibliothek, Vienna), which are copies of original editions, do not possess the merit of sources.

### Editorial Principles

We accept as our basis A, and take into consideration supplements introduced in FE, which could have been made by Chopin, and were accepted by him during lessons. We take into consideration also Chopin's annotations in pupils' copies.

p. 31 *Bar 8 and analog.* R.H. A (→FE→GE,EE) has the following version: [musical notation]. Chopin supplemented it in a similar way in all three pupils' copies, making it possible to recognise the changes as final. Two notes were added on the second crotchet in FES and FEJ (our main text) and only $c^2$ in FED (our variant). In accordance to an account by Chopin's pupil W. von Lenz (see quotations *about the Waltzes...*, prior to the musical text), Chopin added this supplement (in the version given in the main text) also in his copy.

*Bar 23 and analog.* R.H. FE (→GE,EE) overlooked the additional crotchet stem next to $d^2$ in A.
L.H. The variant comes from A. In the proofs of FE (→GE,EE) both *a* were tied. This is the version we give in the main text, in the form in which Chopin usually wrote figures of this type.

*Bars 24 and 92* The mordents were added during the proof-reading of FE (→GE,EE).

p. 32 *Bars 37, 39, 41,43 and analog.* R.H. In A Chopin marked the ornaments (*tr* or ∿) rather carelessly: *tr* occurs certainly in bar 37 and probably in bar 45, while the remaining ornaments resemble mordents (bars 85–152 are marked only as a repetition of bars 17–84). FE (→GE,EE) has *tr* only in bars 37 and 105. In FES Chopin changed three of the printed mordents to trills (in bars 39, 107 and 113). The conclusions are as follows:
— trills should be certainly executed in passages clearly marked by Chopin (in print or pupils' copy) and in analogous ones (bars 37, 39, 45, 47 and analog.),
— we cannot exclude the possibility that corrections in FES signify that Chopin wished to have trills everywhere in this fragment; we note this eventuality by means of *tr* signs in brackets.

*Bars 53, 69, 81 and analog.* The dynamic markings were added during the proof-reading of FE (→GE,EE).

*Bars 55, 59, 63 and analog.* R.H. We give grace-notes in the form of small quavers or semi-quavers as noted in A. In all those bars FE1(→EE) has quavers, GE and FE2 — semiquavers. Originally, Chopin marked those ornaments as mordents (∿), as evidenced by the deletion of those signs in A (one of them, in bar 79, remained overlooked despite the addition of grace-notes).

p. 34 *Bars 121–136 R.H.* In **FED** Chopin added the following voice, an imitative counterpoint of the main melodic line:

This is probably a variegation improvised by Chopin during a pupil's performance and written down upon her request. The execution of both voices with one hand appears to be improbable — the excessive distance would require multiple arpeggiation, unwieldy from the viewpoint of execution and sonority; this is the reason why we treat this insert only as a curiosity, and do not introduce it into the musical text.

p. 35 *Bars 170–171 L.H.* **FEJ** contains unclear signs, possibly fingering numbers. We do not take them into consideration due to the fact that they would be contrary to Chopin's fingering in other sources.

*Bar 174 R.H.* The note $c^1$ in the first chord in **GE**2 (→**GE**3) was arbitrarily (mistakenly?) removed.

# 4. Waltz in F major, Op. 34, no. 3

Sources
[A]   There is no extant autograph.
FE   First French edition, M. Schlesinger (M.S. 2717), Paris December 1838, based on [A] and corrected, presumably by Julian Fontana. It is highly probable that Chopin took part in the proof-reading.
FED, FES, FEJ — as in *Waltz in Eb*, Op. 18.
GE   First German edition, Breitkopf & Härtel (6034), Leipzig December 1838, most probably based on the proofs of **FE**. **GE** includes a number of obvious errors and contains traces of publisher's adjustment; it was not corrected by Chopin. There are copies of **GE** with different covers or the heading.
EE   First English edition, Wessel & C° (W & C° 2282), London December 1838, based on **FE** and including a number of adjustments; it was not corrected by Chopin. There are copies with different covers and title pages.

Editorial Principles
We accept as our basis **FE** and take into consideration Chopin's annotations in pupils' copies.

p. 38 *Bars 95 and 111 R.H.* In those bars the majority of the later collected editions arbitrarily render uniform the sonority of the end of the trill; in some ♯ was added before $d^2$ in bar 95, and in others it was removed in bar 111. The differentiation of this detail could have been intended by Chopin in connection with the different key of the next phrase.

p. 40 *Bar 148 L.H.* The tenth in the source version comprises an unjustified in sound irregularity (the *Waltz* is devoid of other such accompaniment irregularities) and performance complication. The engraver of **FE** probably mistook the note $bb$ for an additional ledger line, thus changing the top note from $d^1$ to $f^1$.

*Bar 152 R.H.* Some of the later collected editions arbitrarily changed the first quaver from $e^1$ to $f^1$.

*Bars 162–163 R.H.* Some of the later collected editions arbitrarily tied the notes $c^1$.

# 5. Waltz in A flat major, Op. 42

Sources
[A]   There is no extant autograph.
FE   First French edition, Pacini (3708), Paris:
FE0   Proof copy of **FE**, based on [A].
FE1   Completed **FE**, corrected and supplemented by Chopin, June 1840. There are copies of **FE**1 with different addresses of the publisher on the covers.
FED, FEJ — as in *Waltz in Eb*, Op. 18.
FEG   Copy of **FE**0 with supplements and corrections added by Chopin, intended as the base for the first German edition (private collections, photocopy rendered available to the editors of the National Edition by Prof. Paul Badura-Skoda of Vienna).
GE1   First German edition, Breitkopf & Härtel (6419), Leipzig July 1840, based on **FEG**. It was not corrected by Chopin. **GE**1 includes a number of errors and contains traces of publisher's adjustments. There are copies of **GE**1 with different prices on the covers.
GE2   Second German edition (same firm and number), after 1852; some of the mistakes of **GE**1 were corrected and a number of arbitrary changes were introduced.
GE3   Revised impression of **GE**2, c. 1867, introducing i.al. an arbitrary change in bar 260.
GE   = **GE**1, **GE**2 and **GE**3.
EE   First English edition, Wessel & C° (W & C° 3559), London June 1840. It is based on a proof copy of **FE** (probably identical with **FE**0) with annotations by Chopin. **EE** was not corrected by the composer and contains traces of publisher's adjustments. There are copies of **EE** with different title pages.

Editorial Principles
Each of the three first editions was based on the proofs of **FE** read by Chopin. The introduced changes as a rule are not the same, although in the majority of cases they could be regarded as mutually supplementary. We introduce them into the text of **FE**0, based directly on [A], while adhering to the following principles:
– Chopin's concurrent corrections in at least two editions are included directly into the main text;
– alterations introduced only into one of the editions are treated facultatively (variants, markings in parentheses); this holds true also for those passages which Chopin corrected differently in various editions. We also take into consideration his annotations in pupils' copies.

p. 41 *Bar 1* The marking $\boldsymbol{p}$ is found in **FEG** (→**GE**) and **EE**, while **Vivace** is only in **EE**.

*Bars 9–39 and analog.* R.H. Some of the later collected editions arbitrarily added lengthening dots to the crotchets of the top voice. For this type of figuration Chopin used both manners of notation, e.g. without dots in *Ballade in G minor*, Op. 23, bar 141 and *Mazurka in B*, Op. 63, no. 1, bars 91–94, and with dots in *Scherzo in E*, Op. 54, bars 249–253 and analog.

*Bar 10 and 182* L.H. On the second and third beat **FE**0 has *Bb-db-g* chords. Chopin changed them into *eb-g* thirds both in **FEG** (→**GE**) and in bases for **FE** and **EE**. The absence of a corresponding change in analogous bar 182 is most probably the result of an omission (when proof-reading Chopin frequently missed the correction of one of several similar passages); consequently, in this bar we also give a corrected version with lighter sounding thirds (this change was introduced already in **GE**2).

p. 42 *Bar 31 and 203* L.H. At the beginning of the bar **FE** has *eb*. In bar 31 Chopin changed it into *Eb* both in **FEG** (→**GE**) and in the base for **EE**. Cf. a similar bass line in *Waltz in C# minor*, Op. 64, no. 2, bars 38-40 and analog. The unchanged *eb* left in analogous bar 203 seems to be the result of Chopin's omission of a correction (see previous comment), and for this reason in the main text we give it in this bar as *Eb*. On the other hand, *Eb* in bar 31 seems to be confirmed by the successive *Eb* in bar 39; therefore, the different shape of the end of the theme in bars 210-212 and, thus, the absence of such a repetition of this note in bar 211 can be considered as an argument justifying the leaving of *eb* in bar 203.

*Bar 38* L.H. On the second and third crotchet **FE** (→**GE**1) has open fifths *ab–eb¹*. This indubitable oversight by the engraver of **FE** (*cf.* bar 30 as well as commentaries to bar 48, 80, 112, 172 and 174) was corrected, probably by Chopin, in the basis for **EE**.

*Bar 44, 52 and analog.* L.H. The main text comes from **FE** (→**GE**). The variants in bar 44, 52, 76 and 84 come from **EE**; this (slightly easier) version could have been added by Chopin while preparing the base for this edition. Since it seems rather unlikely that he intended to differentiate the accompaniment of this part, which recurs upon several occasions, the variants can be applied also in other analogous bars (with the exception of bar 216, due to a different harmonic progression).

*Bar 48, 80, 112 and 172* L.H. On the second beat in **FE**0 there is no *c¹*, probably owing to a mistaken deciphering of [**A**]. Chopin added this note in **FE**G (→**GE**) and in the base for **EE**. In **FE**1 the supplement occurs only in bar 48.

*Bar 49 and analog.* L.H. In those bars the third crotchet in **FE** is the *db¹-eb¹* second. In **FE**G (→**GE**1) Chopin added *g¹* in bar 49, 113 and 269. He undoubtedly intended this change to pertain also to bar 81 and 173 (when correcting frequently recurring fragments Chopin often left some of them uncorrected; in **GE**2 *g¹* was added also in those two bars). Chopin made similar supplements also in the base for **EE**, which has the *db¹-eb¹-g¹* chord in all five passages. In this situation, leaving the original version in **FE** should be regarded as Chopin's inattention.

p. 43

*Bar 58* R.H. On the third crotchet **FE** has a staccato dot below *f²* instead of the note *db²*. This error was corrected by Chopin in the bases for **EE** and **GE** and in **FE**D.

p. 44

*Bar 90* L.H. Some of the later collected editions mistakenly have *Bb* as the third crotchet.

*Bar 91* R.H. **FE** (→**EE**,**GE**1) has the fifth *eb– bb* at the beginning of the bar. **GE**2 changed it arbitrarily to the third *g–bb*.
R.H. The last semiquaver in **FE** (→**EE**) and **FE**G is *db¹-db²*. A comparison with analogous bars 231 and 247 as well as with bar 99 and analog. proves that this is a mistake from **FE**0 omitted in the correction. **GE** has the correct version.

*Bars 95–102* In **FE**G (→**GE**) Chopin added the *f* marking in bar 95. The accent in bar 96 and *cresc.* in bars 97–102 are found only in **EE**.

*Bar 103* R.H. At the beginning of the bar **EE** has, probably mistakenly, the third *g¹-bb¹*.

*Bar 105 and 119* In bar 105 the marking *p* is included only in **FE**G (→**GE**), and in bar 119 – only in **EE**.

*Bars 121–122* R.H. In **GE** there is no tie sustaining *eb¹*.

p. 45

*Bars 139–140* R.H. In **FE** the *eb-c¹* sixth is not sustained to bar

140: . We give the version introduced by

Chopin in **FE**G (→**GE**) and in the base for **EE**.

*Bars 141-142* It may be doubted whether the sustaining of all the components of the chord was Chopin's intention. The absence of a strike at the beginning of the bar is not to be found in any other of his *Waltzes* apart from this passage. In a similar situation the first editions of *Mazurka in D*, Op. 33, no 3, added, contrary to manuscript bases, ties sustaining the bass note in bars 8-9 and 24-25. It is quite possible that also in the *Waltz* in [**A**] only four notes were sustained and one, presumably the bass *Bb*, was supposed to be repeated.
L.H. In **GE**1 the tie sustaining *ab* is overlooked.

*Bars 149 and 157* L.H. We give the different sound of the second crotchet in those bars according to **FE** (→**EE**,**GE**1). **GE**2 and the majority of the later collected editions arbitrarily removed *c¹* in bar 149, and one edition added this note in bar 157.

*Bar 158* R.H. In **FE** (→**EE**) the arpeggio is missing. Chopin added it in **FE**G (although this has not been taken into consideration in **GE**) and in **FE**D.

*Bars 162-164* R.H. In **FE**0 slurs starting with the second beat of bar 162 are missing. In **FE**G (→**GE**) Chopin added three slurs and introduced similar supplements in the base of **EE**. While proof-reading **FE**1 he prolonged the slur starting in bar 152 up to the end of bar 164. Cf. bars 259-260.

*Bar 164* L.H. The variant comes from **FE**0 (→**EE**,**GE**). While correcting **FE**1 Chopin changed *g¹* to *ab¹* in the chord on the second beat, which we give in the main text.

p. 46

*Bar 174* L.H. In **FE** *c¹* is omitted on the second and third beat. Chopin supplemented this absence in **FE**G (→**GE**); **EE** also contains the proper version.

*Bar 196* R.H. At the beginning of the bar **FE** (→**GE**1) has, most probably mistakenly, *c²* (cf. bar 24).

p. 47

*Bars 208–210* The designation *dim.* in bars 208–209 is found only in **EE**, and *sostenuto* in bar 210 — in **EE** and **FE**G (→**GE**).

*Bars 223-226* Chopin added accents in **FE**G (→**GE**).

*Bar 230* The dynamic sign was added by Chopin in **FE**G.

*Bar 231* L.H. The second crotchet in **FE** (→**GE**1) erroneously has the chord *eb–ab–db¹*. The *eb– bb–db¹* in **EE** could be the result of a change by Chopin (this version is also found in **GE**2).

p. 48

*Bar 235* L.H. **GE**2 arbitrarily added *eb¹* to the chord on the third crotchet.

*Bar 236* L.H. At the end of the bar **FE** mistakenly has a quaver rest instead of the bass key. In **GE** the ensuing rhythmic error was removed, reducing the last chord to the value of a quaver. We give the most probable version from **EE**.

*Bar 237* The main text comes from **FE** and **GE**, the variant — from **EE**. In **FE**1 *f* is placed only below the rests, probably mistakenly. In **GE** this marking is omitted despite the fact that Chopin wrote it in **FE**G.

*Bars 240–244* R.H. In **FE**D Chopin marked the *ossia* variant in an abbreviated way. Cf. other variants of this type, consisting in the expansion of the figuration by an octave in *Etude in F minor*, Op. 25, no. 2, bar 67, *Nocturnes in F# minor*, Op. 48, no. 2, bars 113–114 and *in E*, Op. 62, no. 2, bars 68–69 and *Waltz in Ab*, Op. 34, no. 1, bars 163–164 and 167–168. In some of them the concept of a variant could be connected with the range of the piano, expanded in the last years of Chopin's life to *a⁴*.

*Bar 251* L.H. On the third crotchet **GE** erroneously repeated the previous chord.

*Bars 257-261* R.H. Here, **FE**0 has no slurs. The slurs given in the main text were added by Chopin in **FE**G (→**GE**); they are also found in **EE** (apart from the third one in bars 260-261). In the proofs of **FE**1 Chopin wrote a single slur over the whole phrase. Cf. bars 162-164.

*Bar 260* R.H. The *ab²* notes are missing in the last two chords in **FE**0 and **FE**G (→**GE**1→**GE**2). Chopin added them while proof-reading **FE**1 and in the base for **EE**. The chords were also supplemented in **GE**3, but an arbitrary *g²* was introduced in the first.

*Bars 269-289* In **FE**0 these bars do not have any performance markings. Chopin supplemented them in the base for **EE**, in **FE**G and in the proofs of **FE**1, but differently in each of them. Markings without parentheses given in the main text come from **FE**G (→**GE**), those in the footnote — from **FE**1. **EE** has an intermediate version, which in the first part of this fragment (to the beginning of bar 277) is the same as in **FE**1, and in a further part resembles the one in **GE**; this is the reason why in bar 286 and 287 we add to the **GE** version the accents occurring only in **EE**. For other differences between the main text and the version given in the footnote – see commentaries to bars 273 and 281-282.

*Bar 273* L.H. In the bass **FE** and **EE** have only *eb* with no dynamic markings. In **FE**G (→**GE**) Chopin added *Eb* and $\textit{\textbf{ff}}$.

*Bars 281–282* R.H. As the fourth quaver **FE** (→**GE**1) has *ab¹* in bar 281 and the third *ab²-c³* in bar 282; **EE** has a third in both bars. Doubts may arise whether the differentiation of those bars in **FE** and **GE**1, insufficiently justified as regards sonority, is not merely a printing error. On the other hand, the authenticity of the **EE** version is not quite certain, since we cannot exclude a mistake committed by the engraver or a revision made by the publisher. This is why in the main text we take into account both source versions, and in the alternative version of the ending, given in the footnote, next to the **FE** and **GE**1 version we consider yet another solution – single notes (*ab¹* and *ab²*) in both bars; the latter version (in **GE**2) is based on the premise of a mistaken printing of a third instead of a single note in bar 282.

*Bars 284-285* **FE**0 has *ab* as the last quaver in bar 284 and *Ab* at the beginning of bar 285. This is the original version changed by Chopin in **FE**G (→**GE**) and in the proofs of **FE**1 into the version which we give in the main text, and in the base for **EE** – into the version given in the footnote.

## 6. Waltz in D flat major, Op. 64, no. 1

Sources

Ten-bar incipit of the R.H. part (F. Chopin and G. Sand Museum, cell no. 2, Valldemosa)

**As** Sketch of the whole *Waltz* in its original edition (Bibliothèque Nationale, Paris).

**AI, AII, AIII** — three autograph/fair-copies of the not final version, differing in numerous details:

**AI** — two page-long, signed autograph with the marking *Vivace* (Universitätsbibliothek, Bonn),

**AII** — one page-long, unsigned autograph with the marking *Vivace*, offered to Juliette von Caraman in July 1847 (Royal College of Music, London),

**AIII** — two page-long, signed autograph entitled *Waltz*, offered to the Rothschild family (Bibliothèque Nationale, Paris).

**A** Autograph of the final version of the whole opus, serving as the basis for the first French edition (private collection, photocopy in the Fryderyk Chopin Museum, Warsaw).

**FE** First French edition, Brandus et C^ie (B. et C^ie 4743), Paris October 1847, based on **A**. Twice corrected by Chopin, who introduced a number of changes.

**FED, FES** — as in *Waltz Eb*, Op. 18.

**GE**1Db — first German edition of this *Waltz*, Breitkopf & Härtel (7715), Leipzig November 1847 (August 1849?), based on the proofs of **FE** prior to the introduction of final adjustments by Chopin.

**GE**1op — first German edition of the whole Op. 64, Breitkopf & Härtel (7721), Leipzig November 1847, also based on the proofs of **FE** prior to the introduction of last adjustments by Chopin. There are copies with different covers.

**GE**1 = **GE**1Db and **GE**1op. Both forms of **GE**1 differ as regards several details, testifying to their independent and parallel preparation.

There are no traces of Chopin's participation in the production of **GE**1.

**GE**2Db — second German edition of the *Waltz* (same firm and number), including a number of arbitrary changes.

**GE**2op — second German edition of the whole Op. 64 (same firm and number), including a number of arbitrary changes.

**GE**2 = **GE**2Db and **GE**2op. Both forms of **GE**2 preserved their distinctness: the changes introduced therein correspond only partially; the majority of differences between them, taken from **GE**1, were not removed.

**GE**3Db, **GE**4Db — third German edition of the *Waltz*, Breitkopf & Härtel (9619), about 1858, with the text of **GE**2Db differently arranged on the pages, and its later (after 1861), superficially revised, impression.

**GE** = **GE**1, **GE**2, **GE**3Db and **GE**4Db.

**EEC** Earliest English edition, Cramer, Beale & C^ie (4368), London April 1848, reproducing the slightly changed text of **FE**. M. J. E. Brown (Chopin: *An Index to His Works in Chronological Order*, New York 1972) maintains that this was a pirate edition.

**EEW** First English edition, Wessel & C° (W & C° 6321), London September 1848, based on **FE** with small adjustments. Chopin did not take part in its production.

**EE** = **EEC** and **EEW**.

Editorial Principles

We accept as our basis **A** with Chopin's corrections of **FE**. We also take into consideration authentic annotations in pupils' copies (with the exception of certain figures added into **FE**D, whose type face and frequency do not correspond to Chopin's fingering).

p. 50  *Bar 1* R.H. Variant of the beginning of the *Waltz* comes from **FE**D where Chopin added "tr 4 mesures" ("trill 4 bars") next to the first note. Some of the later collected editions arbitrarily added the sign $\textit{\textbf{tr}}$ over the first note of the basic version, given by us in the main text.

*Bars 19 and 91* L.H. Upon the basis of a photocopy of **A**, accessible to the editors of the *National Edition*, it is impossible to say whether Chopin wished to have *ab* on the second and third crotchet of bar 19 (bar 91 is marked only in an abbreviated way as a repetition of bar 19). **FE** (→**GE,EE**) has chords *ab–c¹–gb¹*, but the engraver could have mistaken this bar for bar 17 (cf. commentary to bar 92). Several versions, which in bars 11–12 and 19–20 occur in the accompaniment in **As**, **AI**, **AII** and **AIII**, as well as the crossings in those bars in **A** testify to the fact that up to the very end Chopin sought a version which would be most apt as regards sonority and execution. The uniform form granted to bars 11 and 19 appears to be justified owing to the economy of sound and thinking in categories of pairs of bars (bars 17–18 and 19–20); this is the reason why we give this version as the main one.

*Bars 20 and 92* R.H. In **A** the sign over the third quaver is not quite legible and resembles rather $\textit{\textbf{tr}}$ than ∿. In bar 20 **FE** (→**EE**) has ∿, and **GE** has no ornament, which could suggest that in **FE** it was introduced during the final proof-reading. In bar 92 all editions have $\textit{\textbf{tr}}$ (with the exception of **GE**2op, where this sign was removed). In both bars we accept ∿ owing to the possibility of a correction of bar 20 in **FE**, distinct mordents in **AII** and **AIII**, and performance praxis — in the *molto vivace* tempo both signs denote a mordent.

p. 51  *Bar 34* R.H. The last quaver in **A** is preceded by ♮, removed by Chopin during the proof-reading of **FE** (→**GE,EE**).

*Bar 36 (prima volta)* R.H. **GE**2Db (→**GE**3Db→**GE**4Db) arbitrarily tied *f²* on the third crotchet with the consecutive *f²* in bar 21.
L.H. **GE**1op (→**GE**2op) unnecessarily repeated the sixth *ab–f¹* on the third beat.

Bar 36 (seconda volta) Prior to the third crotchet **A** (→**FE**) has a double bar line and the word *Fine*. This is the remnant of the original end of the *Waltz*, in which bar 76 was succeeded by a repetition of bars 5–36.
R.H. **GE**1op (→**GE**2) erroneously tied $ab^1$ on the third crotchet with the minim in bar 37.

Bars 40–41 R.H. **GE**2 arbitrarily tied $f^2$ over bar line.

Bar 41 L.H. On the second and third crotchet **A** and **GE** have the chords $ab–c^1–gb^1$. During the final correction of **FE** (→**EE**) Chopin removed $c^1$.

Bar 46 L.H. Some of the later collected editions arbitrarily added the note $c^1$ to the second crotchet.

Bar 50 L.H. At the beginning of the bar **A** and **GE** have $c$. During the final proof-reading of **FE** (→**EE**) Chopin changed it to $C$.

Bars 50–51 R.H. In **A** Chopin overlooked ♮ prior to $g^2$ in bar 50 and ♭ prior to $gb^2$ in bar 51. The naturals added by the reviser of **GE**1 before the two notes were not corrected until **GE**4D♭. During the final proof-reading of **FE** (→**EE**) Chopin supplemented the overlooked signs (the text proper does not give rise to doubts also owing to the concurrent versions of **A**I, **A**II and **A**III).

<sup></sup>p. 52 Bars 69–72 R.H. We give the notation of trills according to **A** (→**FE**→**EE**;  **GE** has a notation with wavy lines, as in **A**I). The meaning of the sign **tr**, repeated four times, could give rise to doubts. In the remaining autographs Chopin noted this fragment as follows:

**A**s

**A**I

**A**II

**A**III

Such great variety speaks in favour of the conclusion that all notations signify the same: a continuous trill across four bars.

Bar 92 L.H. In **FE** the first two crotchets were originally the same as in bar 90: $eb$ and $ab–c^1–gb^1$. This mistaken version was reprinted in **GE**. During the final proof-reading of **FE** (→**EE**) Chopin restored the proper accompaniment (the same as in **A**).

Bars 93–95 R.H. The version given in the footnote is an attempted interpretation of the unclear annotation made by Chopin in bar 93 in **FE**S. We have accepted that Chopin wished to achieve variegation by introducing the original (**A**s) version of bars 93 and 95.

<sup></sup>p. 53 Bars 120–121 R.H. Here **FE**D has a not quite legible verbal addition by Chopin. Presumably, this was an on-the-spot lesson directive, e.g. drawing attention to an expanded version of the passage at the end of the *Waltz*: *ici octava* (?).

## 7. Waltz in C sharp minor, Op. 64, no. 2

### Sources

**A**s    Sketch of the whole *Waltz* in the original edition (Bibliothèque de l'Opéra, Paris).

**A**I    Autograph of the not final version, offered to Baroness de Rothschild (Bibliothèque Nationale, Paris).

**A**, **FE** — as in *Waltz in D♭*, Op. 64, no. 1.
**FE**D, **FE**S — as in *Waltz in E♭*, Op. 18.
**GE**1C♯ — first German edition of the *Waltz*, Breitkopf & Härtel (7716), Leipzig November 1847 (August 1849?), based on the proofs of **FE** prior to the introduction of final adjustments by Chopin.
**GE**1op — first German edition of the whole Op. 64, Breitkopf & Härtel (7721), Leipzig November 1847, also based on the proofs of **FE** prior to the introduction of last adjustments by Chopin. There are copies with different covers.
**GE**1 = **GE**1C♯ and **GE**1op. Both forms of **GE**1 differ as regards several details, testifying to their independent and parallel preparation. Superficial proof-reading by Chopin cannot be excluded.
**GE**2op — second German edition of the whole Op. 64 (same firm and number), introducing several arbitrary changes.
**GE**2C♯ — second German edition of the *Waltz*, Breitkopf & Härtel (10097), 1861, with numerous arbitrary supplements and changes. **GE**2C♯ chronologically corresponds only to **GE**4D♭ but in case of the *Waltz in C♯* the existence of essentially differing intermediate impressions or editions may be practically ruled out.
**GE** = **GE**1, **GE**2op and **GE**2C♯.
**EE**C Earliest English edition, Cramer, Beale & Cⁱᵉ (4369), London April 1848, reproducing a slightly changed text of **FE**. M. J. E. Brown (*Chopin: An Index to His Works in Chronological Order*, New York 1972) maintains that this was a pirate edition.
**EE**W First English edition, Wessel & C° (W & C° 6322), London September 1848, based on **FE** with small adjustments. Chopin took no part in its production.
**EE** = **EE**C and **EE**W.

### Editorial Principles
We accept as our basis **A** together with corrections introduced by Chopin into **FE**. We take into consideration also authentic annotations in pupils' copies and changes in **GE**1, possibly made by Chopin.

<sup></sup>p. 54 Bars 19 and 147 L.H. Upon the basis of an accessible photograph the editors of the *National Edition* assume that on the second crotchet **A** has the third $g\#–b\#$. The remaining sources have a chord $d\#–g\#–b\#$. In the main text we give the probable **A** version, which ensures a smoother link with the previous bar; Chopin applied a similar device in bar 7.

Bars 27–28, 29–30 and analog. R.H. The main text comes from **A** (→**FE**→**GE**,**EE**; **GE**2C♯ added a tie sustaining $c\#^2$ in bars 27–28); the variants come from **FE**D. Earlier sources indicate Chopin's hesitations: **A**s does not have ties and **A**I has a tie sustaining $c\#^2$ in bars 27–28 (this tie was also found in **A**, where Chopin deleted it). Cf. *Performance Commentary*.

Bars 31–32 R.H. Analogously to bars 159–160 (see commentary) some of the later collected editions arbitrarily added $g\#^1$ sounded on the third crotchet in bar 31.

Bars 32 and 160 L.H. At the beginning of the bar **A** and **GE** have $c\#$. During the final proof-reading of **FE** (→**EE**) Chopin changed it to $C\#$.

<sup></sup>p. 55 Bars 33 and 161 The sources do not mark a change of tempo at the first appearance of the figurative section (bar 33). Its final recurrence in bar 161 in **A** (→**FE**→**EE**) has **più mosso**, which is absent in **GE**. It seems improbable that Chopin intended a section, which is repeated three times without any changes, to be performed in different tempi. Since in the second half of the *Waltz* (from bar 97) **A** is written in an abbreviated manner, we cannot exclude the possibility that in bar 161 Chopin automatically repeated the marking from bar 97 (where it was required after **più lento** in bar 65). The absence of the marking in **GE** could be then the result of Chopin's proof-reading. This is the reason why in bar 161 we give **più mosso** in brackets. Cf. *Performance Commentary*.

*Bars 34, 42 and analog.* L.H. The presence of notes $c\#^1$ on the second and third crotchet gives rise to doubts. In this type of situation it is very difficult to establish in Chopin's manuscripts whether the eventual inner component of the chord situated on a ledger line really occurs. The photocopy of **A** accessible to the editors of the National Edition renders this task impossible. **FE** (→**EE**) has three-note chords in bars 42, 106, 162 and 170 and sixths in bars 34 and 98. **GE**1 corresponds to **FE**, with the exception of bar 106 where it has sixths. Since repetitions of this section (bars 97–128 and 161–192) in **A** are marked only in an abbreviated manner as repetitions of bars 33–64, the discrepant versions in bar 162 in **FE** (→**GE**1,**EE**) and bar 106 in **GE**1 can be with all certainty regarded as mistaken (in **GE**2op uniformising changes were made in those bars). There remains the question whether the three-note chords in bar 42, 106 and 170 correspond to Chopin's intention. Arguments against this thesis include:
— the exclusive use by Chopin of two-note chords in adjoining bars,
— a concurrent appearance of sixths in bars 34, 50, 58 and analog., identical as regards pitches,
— the replacement in bar 40 of chords occurring in **A**I with sixths found in **A**, which testifies to Chopin's intention to simplify the accompaniment,
— a large probability of an erroneous deciphering of the three-note chords by the engraver of **FE**.
This is the reason why we give sixths as the only text (a version included also in **GE**2C#).

*Bar 45 and analog.* L.H. On the third crotchet **A** and **GE** have the fourth $a–d^1$. During the final proof-reading of **FE** (→**EE**) Chopin added $a^1$ (only in bar 189, owing to an oversight by Chopin or the engraver, this change was not introduced).

p. 56 *Bars 64–96* In **A** and **GE** this section has four flats in the key signature. During the final proof-reading of **FE** (→**EE**) Chopin introduced a notation corresponding to the tonality of this fragment (with five flats).

*Bars 66–67, 70–71, 76–77 and 92–93* R.H. Sources indicate Chopin's hesitations as to the repeating or sustaining of identical notes over bar lines. **A**s, **A**I, **A** (→**FE**→**EE**) and **FE**S do not have ties in those passages. Ties are found in **GE** (possibly added by Chopin in the proofs of **GE**1) and **FE**D (in his handwriting). **GE** also has ties joining $db^3$ in bars 75–76 and 91–92, but their absence in **FE**D shows that either they were added by the reviser of **GE**1 or Chopin subsequently resigned from them.
Two extant pupils' copies testify that Chopin accepted both possibilities in the execution by his pupils. We thus give the version occurring in basic sources with repeated notes as the main version, and the version with ties noted in **FE**D — as the variants.

*Bars 71–72* L.H. In **A** (→**FE**→**GE**1C#,**EE**) there is no tie sustaining $gb^1$. Chopin added it in **FE**S. **GE**1op and **GE**2op do not have both ties in this passage; **GE**2C# contains the correct version.

*Bar 76* L.H. At the beginning of the bar **A** and **GE** have the crotchet $gb$. During the final proof-reading of **FE** (→**EE**) Chopin changed it to the version (accepted by us) with the sustained chord.

*Bars 81–82* R.H. **FE** (→**EE**) do not have the tie sustaining $f^2$, present in **A** and added in **GE**, possibly by Chopin.

*Bar 86* L.H. Some of the later collected editions arbitrarily changed the lower note of the second crotchet from $b$ to $bb$.

*Bars 87–88* L.H. The overwhelming majority of the later collected editions arbitrarily added ties sustaining $c^1–gb^1$.

*Bar 92* During the last proof-reading of **FE** (→**EE**) Chopin added the marking *poco ritenuto*.

p. 57 *Bar 128* L.H. **GE**2C# arbitrarily added $c\#^1$ to the sixth on the second crotchet.

p. 58 *Bars 159–160* R.H. During the last proof-reading of **FE** (→**EE**) Chopin added the crochet $g\#^1$, sounded in bar 159 and sustained as a minim in bar 160. This type of variegation of consecutive repetitions of musical concepts was one of Chopin's favourite composition techniques.

# 8. Waltz in A flat major, Op. 64, no. 3

Sources

**As** Sketch of the whole *Waltz* (Bibliothèque de l'Opéra, Paris).

**A, FE** As in *Waltz in Db*, Op. 64, no. 1.

**FED** As in *Waltz in Eb*, Op. 18.

**GE**1Ab — first German edition of the *Waltz*, Breitkopf & Härtel (7717), Leipzig November 1847 (August 1849?), based on the proofs of **FE** prior to the introduction of final adjustments by Chopin.

**GE**1op — first German edition of the whole Op. 64, Breitkopf & Härtel (7721), Leipzig November 1847, also based on the proofs of **FE** prior to the introduction of last adjustments by Chopin. There are copies with different covers.

**GE**1 = **GE**1Ab and **GE**1op. Both forms of **GE**1 differ as regards several details, testifying to their independent and parallel preparation. Chopin most probably glanced through **GE**1, introducing two slight changes.

**GE**2op — second German edition of the whole Op. 64 (same firm and number), introducing several arbitrary changes.

**GE**2Ab — second German edition of the *Waltz*, Breitkopf & Härtel (10098), 1861, with numerous arbitrary supplements and changes. **GE**2Ab chronologically corresponds only to **GE**4Db but in case of the *Waltz in Ab* the existence of essentially differing intermediate impressions or editions may be practically ruled out.

**GE** = **GE**1, **GE**2op and **GE**2Ab.

**EE** First English edition, Wessel & Cº (W & Cº 6323), London September 1848, based on **FE** with small adjustments. Chopin took no part in its production.

Editorial Principles

We accept as our basis **A** together with corrections introduced by Chopin into **FE** and **GE**1. We take into consideration also authentic annotations in a pupil's copy.

p. 61 *Bar 49* R.H. In **A** the four-quaver motif has the form of $f^1–g^1–g^1–d^1$. Chopin corrected it both in **FE** and, most probably, in **GE**1, but differently in each of them. We give both versions: the **GE** version in the main text, and the **FE** (→**EE**) version in the variant.

p. 62 *Bars 57–60* R.H. Prior to the second quaver in bar 57 **A** has ♮. This means that despite the oversight of corresponding naturals in bars 58–59 Chopin envisaged $d^2$ in the whole four bars. This version was introduced into **GE** via the proofs of **FE**; the former supplemented the missing naturals. During the second proof-reading of **FE** Chopin changed ♮ in bar 57 to ♭, in this way lowering the top notes in bars 57–60 to $db^2$. The change of the L.H. part in bar 60 in **GE**, most probably introduced by Chopin (see below), entitles us to presume that the naturals in bars 58–59 could have been added by him. This is the reason why in the main text we give the **GE** version and in the variant — the **FE** (→**EE**) version.

*Bar 60* L.H. The last chord in **A** (→**FE**→**EE**) is $gb–a–eb^1$ (our variant). In the proofs of **GE**1 it was changed, most likely by Chopin, into $a–eb^1–f^1$.

*Bars 61–62* L.H. **GE**2Ab arbitrarily removed notes $f^1$ from the chords.

*Bars 75–76* L.H. **GE** overlooked the tie sustaining *c*.

*Bars 76–77* R.H. In **A** the minims *g¹* are not tied. The tie occurring in **FE** (→**GE**,**EE**) is probably the outcome of an error made by the engraver. Additional evidence of the fact that Chopin intended to repeat *g¹* in bar 77 is the slur-tenuto over this note.

p. 63

*Bars 97–98, 101–102 and 105–106* R.H. Some of the later collected editions (in bars 97–98 already **GE**2op) arbitrarily added ties sustaining chords over bar lines.

*Bar 107* R.H. In the first chord some of the later collected editions arbitrarily changed the lower note from *f¹* to *g♭¹*.

*Bar 109* During the final proof-reading of **FE** (→**EE**) Chopin added the designation *sostenuto*.

*Bars 109–110 and 125–126* R.H. In **A** there are no ties sustaining *e♭¹*, added by Chopin during the proof-reading of **FE** (→**GE**,**EE**).

p. 64

*Bars 143–144* R.H. In **A** there are no naturals prior to the sixth quaver in bar 143 and the fourth quaver in bar 144. This presumed oversight by Chopin is testified by the presence of naturals in **A**s and their supplementation in the last corrections of **FE** (→**EE**). **GE** added only ♮ raising *d♭²* to *d²* in bar 144.

p. 65

*Bar 152* L.H. Some of the later collected editions arbitrarily supplemented chords on the second and third crotchet, to resemble bar 150.

*Bars 160–164* L.H. **A** and **GE** have the following accompaniment:

During the final proof-reading of **FE** (→**EE**) Chopin removed certain notes, creating an inner melodic line: *g–d♭¹–c¹–a♭–* etc.

*Jan Ekier*
*Paweł Kamiński*

# № 2

*A Madame la Baronne Nathaniel de Rothschild*

**Tempo giusto**

* Patrz *Komentarz wykonawczy.*
*Vide Performance Commentary.*

* Patrz uwaga o tempach w *Komentarzu wykonawczym* i *Komentarz źródłowy* do tego taktu.
  See the remark about the tempi in the *Performance Commentary* and the *Source Commentary* to this bar.

55

58

## № 3

*A Mademoiselle la Comtesse Catherine Branicka*

op. 64 nr 3

**Moderato**

# NATIONAL EDITION OF THE WORKS OF FRYDERYK CHOPIN

Plan of the edition

## Series A. WORKS PUBLISHED DURING CHOPIN'S LIFETIME

| | | |
|---|---|---|
| 1 | **A I** | **Ballades** Opp. 23, 38, 47, 52 |
| 2 | **A II** | **Etudes** Opp. 10, 25, Three Etudes (Méthode des Méthodes) |
| 3 | **A III** | **Impromptus** Opp. 29, 36, 51 |
| 4 | **A IV** | **Mazurkas (A)** Opp. 6, 7, 17, 24, 30, 33, 41, Mazurka in a (Gaillard), Mazurka in a (from the album La France Musicale /Notre Temps/), Opp. 50, 56, 59, 63 |
| 5 | **A V** | **Nocturnes** Opp. 9, 15, 27, 32, 37, 48, 55, 62 |
| 6 | **A VI** | **Polonaises (A)** Opp. 26, 40, 44, 53, 61 |
| 7 | **A VII** | **Preludes** Opp. 28, 45 |
| 8 | **A VIII** | **Rondos** Opp. 1, 5, 16 |
| 9 | **A IX** | **Scherzos** Opp. 20, 31, 39, 54 |
| 10 | **A X** | **Sonatas** Opp. 35, 58 |
| 11 | **A XI** | **Waltzes (A)** Opp. 18, 34, 42, 64 |
| 12 | **A XII** | **Various Works (A)** Variations brillantes Op. 12, Bolero, Tarantella, Allegro de concert, Fantaisie Op. 49, Berceuse, Barcarolle; *supplement* – Variation VI from "Hexameron" |
| 13 | **A XIIIa** | **Concerto in E minor** Op. 11 for piano and orchestra (version for one piano) |
| 14 | **A XIIIb** | **Concerto in F minor** Op. 21 for piano and orchestra (version for one piano) |
| 15 | **A XIVa** | **Concert Works** for piano and orchestra Opp. 2, 13, 14 (version for one piano) |
| 16 | **A XIVb** | **Grande Polonaise in E♭ major** Op. 22 for piano and orchestra (version for one piano) |
| 17 | **A XVa** | **Variations on "Là ci darem" from "Don Giovanni"** Op. 2. Score |
| 18 | **A XVb** | **Concerto in E minor** Op. 11. Score (historical version) |
| 19 | **A XVc** | **Fantasia on Polish Airs** Op. 13. Score |
| 20 | **A XVd** | **Krakowiak** Op. 14. Score |
| 21 | **A XVe** | **Concerto in F minor** Op. 21. Score (historical version) |
| 22 | **A XVf** | **Grande Polonaise in E♭ major** Op. 22. Score |
| 23 | **A XVI** | **Works for Piano and Cello** Polonaise Op. 3, Grand Duo Concertant, Sonata Op. 65 |
| 24 | **A XVII** | **Piano Trio** Op. 8 |

## Series B. WORKS PUBLISHED POSTHUMOUSLY

(The titles in square brackets [] have been reconstructed by the National Edition; the titles in slant marks // are still in use today but are definitely, or very probably, not authentic)

| | | |
|---|---|---|
| 25 | **B I** | **Mazurkas (B)** in B♭, G, a, C, F, G, B♭, A♭, C, a, g, f |
| 26 | **B II** | **Polonaises (B)** in B♭, g, A♭, g♯, d, f, b♭, B♭, G♭ |
| 27 | **B III** | **Waltzes (B)** in E, b, D♭, A♭, e, G♭, A♭, f, a |
| 28 | **B IV** | **Various Works (B)** Variations in E, Sonata in c (Op. 4) |
| 29 | **B V** | **Various Compositions** Funeral March in c, [Variants] /Souvenir de Paganini/, Nocturne in e, Ecossaises in D, G, D♭, Contredanse, [Allegretto], Lento con gran espressione /Nocturne in c♯/, Cantabile in B♭, Presto con leggierezza /Prelude in A♭/, Impromptu in c♯ /Fantaisie-Impromptu/, "Spring" (version for piano), Sostenuto /Waltz in E♭/, Moderato /Feuille d'Album/, Galop Marquis, Nocturne in c |
| 30 | **B VIa** | **Concerto in E minor** Op. 11 for piano and orchestra (version with second piano) |
| 31 | **B VIb** | **Concerto in F minor** Op. 21 for piano and orchestra (version with second piano) |
| 32 | **B VII** | **Concert Works** for piano and orchestra Opp. 2, 13, 14, 22 (version with second piano) |
| 33 | **B VIIIa** | **Concerto in E minor** Op. 11. Score (concert version) |
| 34 | **B VIIIb** | **Concerto in F minor** Op. 21. Score (concert version) |
| 35 | **B IX** | **Rondo in C** for two pianos; **Variations in D** for four hands; *addendum* – working version of Rondo in C (for one piano) |
| 36 | **B X** | **Songs** |

| | | |
|---|---|---|
| 37 | **Supplement** | Compositions partly by Chopin: Hexameron, Mazurkas in F♯, D, D, C, Variations for Flute and Piano; harmonizations of songs and dances: "The Dąbrowski Mazurka", "God who hast embraced Poland" (Largo) Bourrées in G, A, Allegretto in A-major/minor |

# WYDANIE NARODOWE DZIEŁ FRYDERYKA CHOPINA

Plan edycji

## Seria A. UTWORY WYDANE ZA ŻYCIA CHOPINA

## Seria B. UTWORY WYDANE POŚMIERTNIE

(Tytuły w nawiasach kwadratowych [] są tytułami zrekonstruowanymi przez WN, tytuły w nawiasach prostych // są dotychczas używanymi, z pewnością lub dużym prawdopodobieństwem, nieautentycznymi tytułami)

1 **A I**     **Ballady** op. 23, 38, 47, 52

2 **A II**     **Etiudy** op. 10, 25, Trzy Etiudy (Méthode des Méthodes)

3 **A III**     **Impromptus** op. 29, 36, 51

4 **A IV**     **Mazurki (A)** op. 6, 7, 17, 24, 30, 33, 41, Mazurek a (Gaillard), Mazurek a (z albumu La France Musicale /Notre Temps/), op. 50, 56, 59, 63

25 **B I**     **Mazurki (B)** B, G, a, C, F, G, B, As, C, a, g, f

5 **A V**     **Nokturny** op. 9, 15, 27, 32, 37, 48, 55, 62

6 **A VI**     **Polonezy (A)** op. 26, 40, 44, 53, 61

26 **B II**     **Polonezy (B)** B, g, As, gis, d, f, b, B, Ges

7 **A VII**     **Preludia** op. 28, 45

8 **A VIII**     **Ronda** op. 1, 5, 16

9 **A IX**     **Scherza** op. 20, 31, 39, 54

10 **A X**     **Sonaty** op. 35, 58

11 **A XI**     **Walce (A)** op. 18, 34, 42, 64

27 **B III**     **Walce (B)** E, h, Des, As, e, Ges, As, f, a

12 **A XII**     **Dzieła różne (A)** Variations brillantes op. 12, Bolero, Tarantela, Allegro de concert, Fantazja op. 49, Berceuse, Barkarola; *suplement* – Wariacja VI z „Hexameronu"

28 **B IV**     **Dzieła różne (B)** Wariacje E, Sonata c (op. 4)

29 **B V**     **Różne utwory** Marsz żałobny c, [Warianty] /Souvenir de Paganini/, Nokturn e, Ecossaises D, G, Des, Kontredans, [Allegretto], Lento con gran espressione /Nokturn cis/, Cantabile B, Presto con leggierezza /Preludium As/, Impromptu cis /Fantaisie-Impromptu/, „Wiosna" (wersja na fortepian), Sostenuto /Walc Es/, Moderato /Kartka z albumu/, Galop Marquis, Nokturn c

13 **A XIIIa**     **Koncert e-moll** op. 11 na fortepian i orkiestrę (wersja na jeden fortepian)

30 **B VIa**     **Koncert e-moll** op. 11 na fortepian i orkiestrę (wersja z drugim fortepianem)

14 **A XIIIb**     **Koncert f-moll** op. 21 na fortepian i orkiestrę (wersja na jeden fortepian)

31 **B VIb**     **Koncert f-moll** op. 21 na fortepian i orkiestrę (wersja z drugim fortepianem)

15 **A XIVa**     **Utwory koncertowe** na fortepian i orkiestrę op. 2, 13, 14 (wersja na jeden fortepian)

32 **B VII**     **Utwory koncertowe** na fortepian i orkiestrę op. 2, 13, 14, 22 (wersja z drugim fortepianem)

16 **A XIVb**     **Polonez Es-dur** op. 22 na fortepian i orkiestrę (wersja na jeden fortepian)

17 **A XVa**     **Wariacje na temat z *Don Giovanniego* Mozarta** op. 2. Partytura

18 **A XVb**     **Koncert e-moll** op. 11. Partytura (wersja historyczna)

33 **B VIIIa**     **Koncert e-moll** op. 11. Partytura (wersja koncertowa)

19 **A XVc**     **Fantazja na tematy polskie** op. 13. Partytura

20 **A XVd**     **Krakowiak** op. 14. Partytura

21 **A XVe**     **Koncert f-moll** op. 21. Partytura (wersja historyczna)

34 **B VIIIb**     **Koncert f-moll** op. 21. Partytura (wersja koncertowa)

22 **A XVf**     **Polonez Es-dur** op. 22. Partytura

23 **A XVI**     **Utwory na fortepian i wiolonczelę** Polonez op. 3, Grand Duo Concertant, Sonata op. 65

35 **B IX**     **Rondo C-dur** na dwa fortepiany; **Wariacje D-dur** na 4 ręce; *dodatek* – wersja robocza Ronda C-dur (na jeden fortepian)

24 **A XVII**     **Trio na fortepian, skrzypce i wiolonczelę** op. 8

36 **B X**     **Pieśni i piosnki**

37 **Suplement** Utwory częściowego autorstwa Chopina: Hexameron, Mazurki Fis, D, D, C, Wariacje na flet i fortepian; harmonizacje pieśni i tańców: „Mazurek Dąbrowskiego", „Boże, coś Polskę" (Largo), Bourrées G, A, Allegretto A-dur/a-moll

Okładka i opracowanie graficzne · Cover design and graphics: MARIA EKIER
Tłumaczenie angielskie · English translation: ALEKSANDRA RODZIŃSKA-CHOJNOWSKA

Fundacja Wydania Narodowego Dzieł Fryderyka Chopina
ul. Okólnik 2, pok. 405, 00-368 Warszawa
www.chopin-nationaledition.com

Polskie Wydawnictwo Muzyczne SA
al. Krasińskiego 11a, 31-111 Kraków
www.pwm.com.pl

Wyd. II (zrewidowane). Printed in Poland 2023. Drukarnia REGIS Sp. z o.o.
ul. Napoleona 4, 05-230 Kobyłka

ISBN 83-89003-77-5